Chin Up! You Got This!

by

Shakila Stewart

Queen Sierra, (So proud of you!)
You are such a gift to the
world. May you continue to
allow your light to shine.
You are strong, you are beautiful
and you are a Royal daughter of
a king! I love you
Chin Up!

Shakila Stewart

TABLE OF CONTENTS

FOREWORD

LOOK OUT WORLD, HERE COMES SHAKILA, ROOTED AND GROUNDED IN SPIRIT!

So impressed that you have chosen to read *CHIN UP! YOU GOT THIS!* For as they say, it takes one to know one. At a time in your life that may be filled with pressures beyond belief, comes a message from God! Yes, he loves you and loved you all the time. Hard to believe? Right. You were just at times, missing the message while not feeling the messenger. You know the questions, but somehow, or at times, we think that we have all of the answers to those questions. Then, at more especially stressful times, we may push for the answers, but think that we are not speaking loud enough. Ahhhh, HE is there anyway! Always!!! He is guiding, listening, and waiting for you, His child, to bring the pain and or pleasure. He waits patiently because He has such undying belief of greatness for us! That is, even when we think we know it all and halfway believe, I'VE GOT THIS!

This is a powerful memoir of a girl's growth into womanhood. Surrendering to the awesome love of God. Look deeply, Obedience is found to be better than sacrifice! Believe that you are all that He wants you to be ---- right now! Keep on pushing; don't be afraid of His call or His spoken words!

This special memoir truly shows you that belief is powerful! *CHIN UP! YOU GOT THIS!* takes you on a ride from a perceived hell to Hallelujah! You will be inspired far beyond your expectations. There is disbelief, then learning to believe that there really is a GOD! Through it all, success is achievable! The ride gets smoother. Remember, *CHIN UP! YOU GOT THIS!*

MERRI DEE, Legendary Broadcaster and Author of *Life Lessons on Faith, Forgiveness and Grace!!*

ACKNOWLEDGEMENTS

- To my brothers, sisters and nephews: this book is a seed planted for our legacy. I love you with all of my heart. We made it!

- To my Godparents, Tasha Pitchford & Linda Garza: thank you for your unconditional love, prayers and wisdom. I am a powerful woman today because of you two.

- To my grandmother, Della Grigler and my Great- Aunt Willie Grigler: thank you for teaching me how to push forward when the push was hard. I love you and I carry your strength with me wherever I go.

- To my mother the late great, Doris Jean Stewart: words could never express what my heart has always and will forever hold for you. Thank you for giving me the best part of who you are. I treasure my anointing, my authenticity and my power because you were my light, shining ahead.

- To my editor Lora Babalola: girl we did it! Thank you for the long hours, phone calls, dinners, encouraging words and for stepping outside of your comfort zone; you killed it!

- To my proofreading editor, El-Lenor Barbre: thank you for showing up at the right time, and for your diligence, grace and encouragement.

- To all of my friends, uncles, cousins and my Oasis LA church family: thank you for your continued prayers and support.

- To every woman who has a dream or goal: this is for you. Chin Up! You Got This!

Shakila Stewart

PROLOGUE

As a little girl growing up, I had a huge imagination. I was born a "Dreamah!" (Dreamah™ is a character inspired by my life story. She is not raised by her parents, yet she continues to have a positive outlook on life). I had dreams of moving from the Windy City, Chicago, Illinois to the hills of Hollywood, California, and becoming a famous supermodel and actress. I wanted to wear the most beautiful and expensive gowns on the red carpet, sign autographs, eat at the finest restaurants, get picked up in limousines, and blow kisses to the world while boarding my private jet. In my youthful mind, I was a combination of Princess Diana, Janet Jackson, and Paris Hilton, haha. I just knew that I was going to be a star, and no one could tell me anything differently. Every night I would lay in my bed, write inside my journal and listen to my heart. My heart told me that I was going to be a television star who would win an Oscar, so that's where I put all of my life focus. Yet, with such a huge imagination, I also had this hole in my heart and plenty reminders that made me feel like I wasn't worthy enough for my dreams to come true. I thought that there was so much drama and disappointment in my life that my dreams were so out of reach. From being born to teen parents and being in the foster care system, to eventually having to raise my siblings at the tender age of twenty-six, at times, I wasn't sure if it was even worth having a dream.

My experiences left me feeling unworthy, rejected, and lonely. I often asked myself were my dreams possible and were they worthy enough to pursue? In truth, the deeper question I needed to ask were, am I worthy enough for my dreams to come true? And if my dreams did come true, was this going to fix my broken heart? Would achieving my dreams make up for the shame I felt of not being raised by my parents? Would the feelings of my parents not wanting me go away? What I really needed was someone to sit me down and say, ***"Shakila, you are significant. You are loved, important, and extremely special. Your circumstance and environment do not define you."***

Overtime, I discovered that yes, I AM WORTHY and yes, my DREAMS ARE POSSIBLE and WORTH PURSUING because no matter what obstacles I have gone through, I have always conquered them. Besides, these dreams were in my heart and they weren't going anywhere. I had to keep telling myself, "I can break generational curses, I can be great, but it's going to take fight, perseverance and a new mind-set." Generational curses are negative behavioral patterns that repeat throughout the generations in a family if they are left unaddressed and unchecked.

The funny thing is that all of my life I thought that my dream was going to bring all of the healing and restoration I ever needed, but the truth is, it has been the Lord who has drastically changed my life for the better. I put a lot of energy into becoming successful and achieving my dream thinking that it would be the key to filling the void of not being raised by my parents.

However, the truth is nothing will fill that void but Christ. I had to get real with myself and ask myself the hard questions, *"What is my motivation for going after my dreams? Is it for acceptance? Is it for love?"* In reality, there was nothing wrong with my dreams or having them, the problem was that I thought accomplishments would bring me healing, and it doesn't. Going after my dream was me trying to prove a point to people, that I was successful, that I was enough, that I was on top, and most importantly, that my issues didn't define me. As you read this book, I want you to discover how to walk into developing a positive identity, the power of having a dream, and the blessing that comes along with surrendering what you want for what God wants for you. Step into your big girl shoes and let's go on an amazing quest toward your destiny; Chin Up, you got this, Walk This Way!

CHAPTER ONE

Dreamah

Growing up, my biological parents didn't raise me; I was adopted. Prior to adoption, I was in foster care from ages five to eight. When my biological mother had me, she was sixteen and my father was fifteen (they were definitely too young to be having sex, lol). Immediately after I was born at Michael Reese Hospital in Chicago, Illinois, my mother gave me to my

5

grandmother and she was the one to raise me until I was five years old. Grandma was so loving towards me. I was her baby and she had me spoiled rotten. I was so spoiled by her that once, when I was about three years old, I would not stop crying for days so she finally took me to the emergency room to see why. The doctor simply told her nothing is wrong with this baby, "She sounds like she is just spoiled!" Oh I loved my grandma so much; I simply wanted all of her attention and would cry until I got it! I remember sitting on the living room floor drinking milk, watching the Oprah Winfrey Show and her favorite soap operas, All My Children and One Life to Live, with her every day. On Sundays we would walk to a Baptist church down the street from our apartment and take communion. I would see all the older ladies wearing their all white dresses and fancy hats. She would never let us miss a Sunday.

Although my grandmother primarily raised me, my mother would still help Grandma take care of me. As a teen mom, she dropped out of school and began to hustle to help provide for me. We lived in the Ida B. Wells projects in Chicago and all she saw around her growing up were drug dealers, gangsters and hustlers. My mom was also very ambitious, I would say she was a "dreamah", and all she really wanted was a better life for herself, so she did it the best way she knew how by becoming a hustler.

When I was five, my grandmother had a boyfriend who was around often and was someone I knew very well. He would sing Sam Cooke songs, could answer any question on Jeopardy, and could play the guitar. One day she went to the store and left me at home with him, but this time was different. I remember I was wearing blue jeans and a green sweater. My hair was in a ponytail and he had been swinging and tickling me all day. I remember I was in the bed when he started kissing on me and he began unbuttoning my pants. I just remained still there next to him when all of a sudden he said, "Get your ass up and get out of here!" As I look back, I know God had protected me. God had His hands over my life even as a young child. The next morning I told my grandmother what happened right in front of his face. She was lying in her bed and he was sitting on the sofa in her room. Of course he denied it. My grandmother called the police and took me to the police station to make a report. The next thing I know, I was with my uncle Jerry (my mom's brother who was fourteen at the time) in a courtroom with two ladies and they were asking us if we wanted to stay with my grandma. I said no, because in my five-year-old mind, I thought it meant I had the option to stay with my cousins who lived in the suburbs instead. However, the court took it a different way. My grandmother was so furious; she didn't understand what had transpired. How was I to know, that answer was going to lead me to foster care and change the course of my life?

Being in foster care was okay as long as my uncle was there with me. We were on the west side of Chicago and the gangs were deeply infested. Being a fourteen-year-old black male in the foster care system was highly volatile because unfortunately, families did not want teenagers, let alone teenage boys of his description. Over the course of time, he ran away and the system let him go.

In the foster care home without my uncle, I felt alone in this new place and scared around all these new people. Be that as it may, it was a very nice home. It was a five-bedroom house with a basement and a garage. It was quite beautiful. Looking back, I realized God always made sure that I had the best. The family was very kind. It was an older woman, her daughter and her daughter's three kids that lived there. They were a very structured family. We ate breakfast, lunch and dinner at the same time every day and we could only eat fast food once a month if we earned it by cleaning up after ourselves, doing our chores and behaving in school. Our "outside clothes" for the playground and our "school clothes", were separate. We went to the Farmer's Market on Saturday mornings and then we would come home to get our hair washed and braided for Sundays when we would go to church. They were very structured compared to my family because I came from a partying family. Friday nights around my biological family was James Brown, Muddy Waters, Hauling Wolf, food and my grandmother and her sisters telling the kids to get in the center of the floor and "dance your butt off". Yes, foster care was very different from grandma's house.

Although I was in foster care with a great family, I missed my grandmother so much. At the foster home you could go on visits with your real family with supervision and I would see Grandma once a month. We would go to the park, hug and kiss each other and I would eat so much candy with her. We would lie on the grass and she would ask me how I was doing and we would laugh and talk about everything. I would have a complete fit when it was time to leave her and I would cry nonstop. It was so hard to leave someone who loved you so much and you loved her back just the same. I remember a day after visiting with Grandma, I went back to the foster home and I was crying uncontrollably. The social worker dropped me off; I ran upstairs, jumped on my twin bed and I could not stop crying. Mrs. Martha, the lady who had custody of me, sat next to me, hugged me and asked, "What's wrong sweetie?" and I said "I don't want to go back with my grandmother!" and she said, "We love you Shakila and you don't have to go anywhere you don't want to go. You are so loved here!" I lied to her because I didn't want to hurt her feelings, but the truth was that I really wanted my grandmother. That night I got on my knees and prayed before bed, "God, I am a good girl, I love everyone even the devil (yes, I said it! I was a desperate five-year-old who wanted her grandmother). Can you please send me back home to my grandma? Amen." Grandma planted the seed of prayer in me, and for the first time, I really used it so I could get back to her.

Although I lied to my foster mother about wanting to see my grandmother, I was still able to visit. Sometimes, my cousins would come during my visits with her as well. I would still have a fit after every visit when it was time to leave her. I remember one particular day, after a visit with my grandmother, quite poignantly. It was in the middle of the school day and the social worker dropped me off at school. He was taking me upstairs and I just screamed and started pulling away from him. I couldn't utter the words that I wanted my grandmother and that I didn't want to go to class. I gave him such a hard time that the school security guard came and walked me to my classroom. She announced to the teacher, in front of the entire class, "Shakila just got dropped off by the Department of Children and Family Services". I felt labeled and humiliated. As I walked toward my seat, my teacher called me to her desk, put me on her lap, and said, "Shakila, I didn't know that you were in foster care". She gave me a hug and sent me back to my seat; that was what I really needed in that moment, a hug to know that everything was going to be ok. She did not make a big deal about receiving that information. She made certain to pay a bit more attention to me during class, and did it in such a way that my peers did not feel disconnected or ignored.

Having to go back to school while visiting my grandmother and being in foster care, were all *chin up, shoulders back* moments for me because I had to sit in class, be strong, pay attention to my teacher and learn the curriculum as if nothing was wrong or as if my heart wasn't hurting. I had to encourage myself at times and say, " You got this", everything is going to be ok, not knowing if I would ever move back with my grandmother.

11

Having been in the role of a teacher myself, I understand not all children are self-motivated and able to push themselves to achieve in the classroom beyond their pain. That is why I believe teachers must pay attention to students, beyond the curriculum, and really strive to build personal relationships with them. Teachers have the power to shape and mold their student's identity and emotions as well as their dreams. My teacher went the extra mile to show me empathy when I needed it, which made it easier for me to deal with pain while going to school as well.

Prayer Works:

I can remember the day that I left the foster home; I was eight years old. I packed all of my clothes in a black garbage bag and I really wanted to take my bike, but I had to leave it there. I was a little salty about that, but I didn't care that much because I was going home with my family. It took time, but God answered my prayer. I had faith that I wanted to get back to my family and my grandmother, so I prayed. At this moment I knew prayer worked and moving forward, this would be the weapon I used to overcome any obstacle in my life.

Eventually, my great Aunt Doris, whom I call Aunti, adopted me. Although being adopted was the best thing that has ever happened to me, I always felt that I wasn't good enough or that my dreams weren't going to come true because I wasn't raised by my biological parents. This was a constant battle that I had to fight while pursuing my dreams. It was this overbearing feeling of never feeling worthy or good enough no matter what circumstances, obstacles, or opportunities presented themselves.

I distinctly remember when and where my feeling of unworthiness began. It all started when I was in fourth grade. It was silent reading time and one of the girls in my class and I started arguing. I must have been winning because she pulled up on the offensive end and said, "That's why you don't have a family!" and I replied saying, "What do you mean I don't have a family?" My friend then stepped in and said, "Mrs. Corn told the class that your family isn't your real family and that you were adopted." In that moment, I was so embarrassed and wanted to burst into tears. I immediately walked up to my teacher's desk and asked her why she told the class that personal information about me, and all she said was, "I don't know much about your family." I went home and told Auntie what happened and she spoke to my teacher the next day. But, from that moment on, I felt that being adopted was a bad thing and was how the world would see me, as the girl with no family, and soon enough, that's how I began to see myself.

As teachers, we have influence over the way children see themselves, so we have to be very careful with the words that we say to them. Proverbs 18:21 says, "Life and death are in the power of the tongue." We can use our tongue to speak life or death, and at that moment my teacher spoke death to my self-esteem. My peers didn't need to know that I was adopted, unless I told them and when I confronted my teacher about it, her response was as if she didn't care about my feelings and consequently this affected my esteem.

It is just as important for teacher's to consider students' family circumstances and their feelings just as much as they consider the curriculum. My teacher could have spoken life to me at that moment, maybe even apologized or asked me about my feelings or maybe not have said anything at all.

However, what the enemy meant for evil, God turned it around for my good. This is why I am so passionate about speaking life into women and youth today because I know the power of words. Although my teacher planted this seed, somewhere in my heart I knew that God was saying that I was special. I just needed someone or something to confirm it.

CHAPTER TWO

The Confirmation: I Am Special

God is faithful. When I was nine years old, He confirmed it in such a way that only a small child would understand that she was special and had a purpose. It was Black History Month; I was sitting in the dining room on the couch reading a book about the media mogul, Oprah Winfrey, when I discovered that she and I shared the same birthday. I started screaming and jumping up and down before I ran to the bathroom to exclaim to my older cousin, "Guess what?! I share the same birthday as Oprah!" She smiled and gave me a big hug, clearly understanding the magnitude of this treasured information. That moment was my first confirmation and wink from God that I was special and worthy enough for my dreams to come true. After that discovery, I told myself every day that I was special, and of course everyone who I met from that day on knew that Oprah and I shared the same birthday, January 29th! It made me feel so special sharing the same birthday as Oprah, because for me, this certified in my mind that I had something in common with someone who was successful and my identity was no longer just an orphan.

This really inspired me to Dream. I told myself that I was going to be a model, actress and director. I began writing plays, songs, and creating choreography, for my cousins, friends and my church. During my middle school years, I performed plays at school and my teachers would always tell me that I was a natural at performing. One night at church, a pastor prayed for me and he told me, "God is going to open a door for you to act, but when He does, don't forget about Him!" I promised that I would not.

I was very bold and confident about telling people my dream and career interests, and by seventeen, one of my dreams finally came true. I was driving in the car listening to the radio, and I heard a commercial headline announcing that they were auditioning print models for a national commercial for an African American hairline, Luster's Inc. I immediately got excited and went to audition. Five hundred people auditioned and only seven girls were chosen. Can you guess who one of the seven girls was? I was! I could not believe that I got it! I was so excited and this was my first professional job that I got a paycheck for being a model. One secret about the magazine industry is that when you are in the magazine, you never know the exact date the project is going to be published. I was on billboards, in magazines, and people were calling me saying, "I saw your picture in this store." It's funny because the first time I saw myself in a magazine, I was eating lunch in the school cafeteria and one of my friends came to me with a copy of *Black Sophisticated Hair* and said, "Look Shakila! You're in this magazine." Booking that job with Luster's Inc. as a hair model gave me the confidence to audition for John Robert Powers Modeling and Acting school in Chicago, and I got in!!

Attending John Robert Powers gave me the professional industry experience training that I needed. I was driving to downtown Chicago by myself, paying for parking, dressing

17

professionally in skirts, heels and blazers, carrying a portfolio with my resume, and learning how to introduce myself to entertainment industry professionals. I felt so grown.

During my training at John Robert Powers, we went through a ten-week modeling and acting training program. At the end of the ten weeks, each student could audition to win a trip to fly to Hollywood, CA to meet with an agency and get discovered to be on television! At this point, all I ever wanted to do was go to Hollywood, so I was beyond hyped. Going to Hollywood meant that I was no longer going to be labeled an orphan; I was going to be the one in my family to make it. I was going to make up for all of the negative things that had happened in my life and break the generational curses. I was putting a lot of pressure on myself, but it didn't matter because this was the moment I had been waiting for. And what do you know? I auditioned and made it! Things were looking up for me. I was no longer only this girl who was once in foster care and adopted. I was a superstar and I was going to Hollywood. I was walking with my chin up, my shoulders back, my face radiating happiness and my joyful heart screaming, "I got this!"

CHAPTER THREE

Hollywood, Don't Pass Me By

When I got to Hollywood, the competition was fierce. The convention was huge with talent from all over the world looking to get discovered, and let me tell you, these people did not come to play. There were beautiful girls and talent everywhere. From their hairstyles to their bodies and outfits…it just got real. I can remember one of our instructors telling us during training, "Your parents and family members are telling you that you are sooo cute, but when you get to Hollywood it's another story!" He was right. It was then that I realized the reality of achieving my dreams wasn't going to be as easy as I thought. There was so much competition and so much work that had to be done. I had gotten the modeling job and admittance into the modeling school so smoothly before, I just assumed that everything else was going to come just as easily. All of the lessons that I learned at John Robert Powers in Chicago, I had to perfect and do it all ten times better in Hollywood: wardrobe, hair, make-up and networking. I competed in both the make-up and headshot introduction competition, and out of five thousand contestants, I won first runner up in both categories! I was so ecstatic about that, but ultimately my goal was to be on television. One talent agency wanted me to relocate from Chicago to Hollywood, but it did not come with any guaranteed movie or television deals; nothing was promised. He just said that he could work with me if I was in Hollywood.

In that moment, I learned that **experiencing your dream is a totally different feeling from imagining your dream.** I was in Hollywood, the place that I always wanted to be, and I was left with two choices: relocate so that I could *possibly* be on television and my dream could come true or go back to Chicago and go to college.

The many stories I had read about helped me understand that there were so many sacrifices that come with living your dreams, and now I was experiencing it firsthand. When I really thought about it, I knew deep in my heart that I was not ready to leave my family and friends in Chicago, plus, I still wanted to attend college. Weighing those options, I decided to go home, which made my very first trip to Hollywood bittersweet. I didn't get an agent, I wasn't discovered, and I wasn't in any movies. I felt defeated. I hadn't accomplished what I set out to do. It seemed I was not going to rescue my family and now I was left wondering if maybe my teacher had been right all those years ago.

Experiencing just a little taste of Hollywood, I got a glimpse of the reality of the sacrifices, discipline and hard work that it was going to take to achieve my dreams. Was I really ready?

Home sweet home:

Before I knew it, those relentless thoughts started creeping right back in. "*Shakila, you're not good enough, you know you don't have what it takes"*...and so on. This was just the beginning of my battle toward finding my identity and self-worth. I put all of my energy and sense of self into accomplishing my goals and when that was not happening, I felt like was failing.

When I got back to Chicago, I didn't discuss in detail with my family or friends what happened in California, I just left it alone. I told them things didn't work out as planned and that was that. Besides, it was my senior year of high school, it was graduation season and I was the first one in my family going to college. I had been accepted to Northern Illinois University. Thankfully, I had other things occupying my mind that brought me some joy and satisfaction. I didn't feel like such a failure anymore, I was still breaking generational curses, and at the least I would still be helping my family.

My Hollywood experience left me feeling that maybe I needed a break from performing. Clearly it wasn't the right timing or, possibly, not what I should be doing altogether. Therefore, I decided to major in Sociology instead of continuing going down the Performing Arts career path, though that didn't last too long. During the first semester, my school was having auditions for a play and I of course auditioned. I felt I was home, being on that stage, like it was the place where I belonged. After the audition, I changed my major right away from Sociology to Theatre, and although I still wanted to be an actress and win an Oscar, I did not major in Theatre Performance alone, my emphasis was Playwriting, Directing and Storytelling. Going to Hollywood exposed me to how challenging it was just to be an actress. I didn't want anybody to tell me when and where I could and should perform. I discovered I could create my own stories and that there was just as much power behind the scenes. And if I ever wanted to be on stage, I could be.

I did not stop there; I was also really into dance in college. I created praise dances for our student showcase performances and fundraising events, and soon, I became known around campus for doing praise dance performances. One unique opportunity that praise dancing awarded me was being able to fly out to California and perform at the Staples Center for the Azusa Street Centennial. It was broadcasted on TBN in celebration of a mighty move of God that happened on Azuza Street in California in 1906, known as the "Pentecostal Movement". It was a rebirth of "hunger for the Lord" that continues to be expressed in congregations across denominational lines. I did not know it then, but this opportunity ignited something in me. I felt that God was telling me that my talents were going to be used for His glory. I believe God was introducing His purpose for me.

CHAPTER FOUR

Condemnation

College allowed so much freedom and independence and now I understood why Aunti was so strict on me in high school. In high school I was a model, cheerleader, and I was dating football and basketball players. My high school boyfriend was two years older than me, so Aunti would only allow me to talk on the phone with him for fifteen minutes a day after school. If he and I went out on a date, she would make sure one of my cousins would come along with us. She wanted to make certain I had a strong sense of self-respect and responsibility.

Every Saturday morning Aunti would go to the grocery store and Walmart to get cleaning products and household items. Before she got back home, I'd have to have the bathroom, kitchen and living room cleaned before she stepped one foot through that door. It especially had to be done if I wanted to go hang out with my friends or go to a party that night. I remember one of the biggest high school parties was a pajama party at a hotel (No, it wasn't anything bad, they were just cute outfits, I swear!). Aunti said that I could not go because respectable girls did not do things like that; I was furious with her for that. Everyone at my school went to that party. The next day at church I had an attitude and she told everyone that I was mad because I didn't go to the "hotel party" so, understandably, now I was furious and insulted! Everyone was telling me "It's okay Shakila, you have to respect yourself as a lady." That was how Aunti was; she just wanted the best for me. I now understand that one of the main ways she felt she could teach me respect and protect me was by making sure I wasn't out there being fast.

For the most part, if I cleaned up my room and kept the house clean, Aunti would let me go hang out with my friends. Before we would go outside, wearing our heels and short skirts, she would pray over all of us before we left the house. She would even put blessed oil over our heads and say, "Cover and protect them with your blood, Jesus!" I'm so glad she did because we were always hanging out with boys, and even though we were not having sex with them, everyone thought we were. I was saving myself for marriage; at least, my goal was to save myself for marriage.

My baby brother was born when I was in high school so I knew what it was like to have a newborn baby around; he was my birth control. I would have to fix bottles, change his diapers, rock him to sleep at night, and sometimes, take him to basketball and football games with me. He was truly like my baby, so I knew that I wasn't ready for any children. Besides, Aunti made it very clear: "Shakila, you better not bring no babies in this house! I'm not raising nobody's kids." She drilled this speech into me every Saturday morning, nonstop. So I knew that I couldn't bring any babies in the house or I was going to get it.

When it was time to graduate high school and go to college, I was so excited. I was like, "Yes, I'm about to be free!"

I had a great graduation party at my godparents' house on the lake. We had boat rides, music, dancing, and kayaking, and I got so many gifts. It was the time of my life. When it was finally time for me to leave for college, Aunti was sad to let me go. She said a testimony in church before I left saying, "Shakila is going off to college. The scripture that I will stand on is Proverbs 3:5-6, 'Trust in the Lord with all of your heart and lean not to your own understanding. In all your ways acknowledge God and He will make your paths straight.'" She was so proud of me, but I wasn't trying to hear that. I was ready to go to college and live my best life with no plans to come back home at all. I was going to find my husband and be on my way. I thought to myself, "I got this!" I just knew that I knew what I was doing.

The day I was leaving for college, all of my family and some church members came over to say farewell. All I was thinking about was my freedom. When Aunti dropped me off, she gave me some cash inside an envelope and kissed me goodbye. As soon as she drove off, I was ready, and within three hours, my roommate and I were at a party. I didn't even unpack; we were just on our way. I had my hair in gold and brown micro braids (thinking I was Beyoncé) and had on a glitter leopard tank top, some blue Donna Karen Jeans and clear and blue jean high-heeled shoes to match. I thought I was the business. My college was known as a "party school". For Homecoming we would have music artists like Ludacris, Nelly, and the Black Eyed Peas perform at our events. Every weekend, my girls and I had something to do. I joined a hip-hop dance team on campus called Flawless. We would perform at events on campus wearing these little short shorts and tank tops. We thought that we were too cute. We would go to comedy shows, fashion shows and parties all the time. It was a blast!

I began dating the captain of the football team. He was a senior and I was a freshman. I told Aunti and she said "Oh, so you on that tip again dating those athletes." Haha, she really didn't play, but I didn't care. My mind was made up; I just knew I knew what I was doing!

He would let me drive his car, have roses delivered to my room, and buy me chocolates. I wore heels to class every day, so he was so thoughtful and bought me a foot massager. And before he went to away games, he would visit me in my dorm room. Things were going great; I was falling in love with college and living my best life.

It's so funny because the first thing guys ask you to do in college is spend the night. And one night, I finally had sex with him. I felt horrible. I had discussed with him before how important it was for me to wait until I was married to have sex. I had put so much pressure on myself to be perfect. When I lost my virginity I was so ashamed and I thought that God didn't love me anymore. I didn't have anyone to talk to about it and I definitely wasn't going to talk to Aunti about it. I had an image to uphold and I didn't want to tell any of my mentors at church. I didn't feel that I could tell any of my friends because I was too prideful. I decided not to tell anyone because I didn't want to ruin my "good girl" appearance. That was one of my biggest mistakes at the time. Now, I would advise anyone who grew up in a strict Christian home or church to have someone you can trust to talk to because keeping that secret inside was hurting me more than I realized.

A few months later the guy and I broke up. He started acting funny, not answering the phone, we didn't go out as much, and it was his senior year of college so he became "focused" on his future. I felt so guilty; I was holding the hurt and pain inside. I would go home and visit family and church, and I knew they could feel something was going on. But no one ever said anything *to* me, just *about* me. I was sad and I began to engage in self-sabotaging behavior, I just knew I had disappointed God and

He didn't love me anymore. Soon enough, I began settling into new relationships. I didn't think that I deserved the best anymore. I started dating another guy over the span of three years. He had money and would buy me anything that I wanted. He would also cheat on me, have baby mommas, do all sorts of disrespectful things, and I took him back every single time. I stayed with him all those years because I wanted him to see that I was the best woman for him. That I was the best pick and the one he needed. But he didn't see that. One day I realized I dealt with his cheating for three years too long and I got fed up. After a nice dinner, he dropped me off at home and I was just tired of him and the constant disrespect. I blocked him and went on a fast for six days. I prayed and cried out to God to please deliver me from him, to help me move on. It was so hard; there was a point where I thought that I would never get over him. My emotional deliverance came December 14, 2004 and from that day on, I never looked back. No matter how many times he tried to call, come over, go out to dinner, I did not look back, by the grace of God. I was tired and if he couldn't see my worth, that was on him. I wanted someone who was loyal. The breakup happened around my winter break, so fortunately, I was able to be around my family and friends, which made things a little bit easier. Plus, he didn't go to my school so I didn't have to see him. After that, I just got focused.

There was a hard lesson I am thankful to have learned. Just because you're not a virgin doesn't mean God loves you any less. Just because you're a virgin doesn't mean that you're perfect. The only thing that will keep you in college is the word of God. You need to stay in the word and know God's opinion about sex. Always remember that God made the first move with you. He died on the cross for your sins before you even asked for forgiveness. He desires a relationship with you and whatever is hindering that, He will remove. He will give you the strength to let it go.

CHAPTER FIVE

The Wiz

When I was nineteen years old, two weeks before my twentieth birthday, my biological mother passed away. I had never told anyone this, but I had always dreamed that she would be in my life. I never prayed about it or mentioned it to any of my friends or family, it was just something that I wanted. It was a dream that I wished wasn't just a dream. I was so hurt. My heart was broken

33

because deep down I thought that we were going to be a family one day, and when she died, all hope was gone.

I remember the last conversation that I had with her. After visiting her in the hospital, I was driving back to school continuing our conversation on the phone. My youth director from church was visiting her as well. She was laughing and making jokes, and she just had confidence out of this world. When I got to school I called her back and said, "Mom you're an angel and you are so special to God. And the reason that I know that you're special is because you have amazing children." I said "I love you mom" and we hung up the phone. Two weeks later, I was at school on my way to class when my sister Tanasia called me and said, "She's gone!" I was confused and said, "what do you mean that she's gone?" That's when she said the words I never wanted to hear, "Our mom died." I just hung up the phone in disbelief, took a deep breath and went to my room. The first thing that came to my mind was that God wasn't playing. I have to get it together. I told my roommate and she hugged me as I cried. I really didn't know what to do or how to react. This was the first person who was close to me that died and there were a lot of emotions I had to deal with. Her funeral was packed with so many people and they had great things to say about her. They called her "the Wiz" because of her brilliance and I really needed to remember that.

I know Jesus for myself now:

When I got back to school, I was miserable. I didn't know what was going on in my life. I was still feeling bad about losing my virginity, the break up with my boyfriend and now my mom was gone. I remember going back to school feeling depressed and lonely. I didn't have any peace and I couldn't focus in class, so I decided to see a college therapist. I remember sitting down in her office and I explained to her that my mom had just passed and that I had this aching feeling and I couldn't find the words to describe it. But as I left, I felt that she didn't really help me. So I just did the only thing that I knew to do. I came home, pulled out my journal and I wrote a letter to God. I said, "Jesus, I don't know what's going on in my life right now, but I need you to deliver me. For the next month I'm going to come home and worship you more than I focus on my problems because nothing else is helping me."

The greatest thing about God is that He knows exactly what's going on before you tell Him. He knows where the pain is, how it feels, and the best part, how to remove it. He gave me something the therapist could never give me: healing and peace.

Every day after school I would drop my books, get on my knees and pray for one hour saying, "Thank you, Jesus; thank you, Jesus!" For one hour, non-stop I would just praise God and not ask him for anything. God just began to heal me, and in that moment, I knew that I was loved by God. I knew that He was nice, loving and kind. He showed me that He was the bread of life in my life and that he would fill every void. I finally felt so whole and complete. Spending time in prayer with God helped build my faith. My relationship was building with Him and I felt so much peace, joy, and love I knew that I was going to be okay. It is almost indescribable. I learned that **you can make it in life without your parents, but you cannot make it in this world without God**. His word says, "I am the bread of life and he who comes to me shall never hunger or thirst for anything else" (John 6:35). After receiving this revelation, God became my everything. I was so excited about the things that God did for me that I wrote a play called, "Never Forsaken" about a woman who had kidney failure and the only match for her was her biological mother. It was a story of healing, hope and restoration. It was based on my testimony of God never forsaking me and always keeping His promise. Writing this play brought so much healing to the death of my biological mother, and seeing my work on stage and getting praised by my college professors and peers was beautiful. I also began to praise dance around campus to a song by Yolanda Adams, called "In the midst of it all", just declaring to people how God brought me through hard trials and how God kept me through it all. Everyone loved to see me dance to this song because they knew all of the moves were coming from my heart to give God glory and to let others know that God loved them too.

The Woman at the Well:

During this time, God started to speak to me about a story in the bible about the Woman at the Well (John 4). She was a woman who was thirsty and seeking after something and getting the void filled from men. She had 5 husbands and was now living with her boyfriend. She then had a special encounter with Jesus and it changed her life forever.

She was at the well getting water when Jesus came by and asked her for a drink. She asked Him how could He ask her for a drink since He was a Jew and she, a Samaritan. Back in those days, Jewish people did not speak to Samaritans, especially not women, so Jesus was already breaking the rules so that this woman could receive her breakthrough. "The Samaritan woman said, 'You are a Jew and I am a Samaritan woman. How can you ask me for a drink?' Jesus said 'If you knew the gift of God and who it is that is asking you for a drink you would have asked him, and He would have given you living water.' 'Sir you have nothing to draw with and the well is deep. Where can you get this living water? Are you greater than our brother Jacob, who gave us the well and drank from it himself?' Jesus answered, 'Anyone who drinks this water will be thirsty again, but whoever drinks the water I give will never thirst. Indeed, the water I give him will become in them a spring of water welling up to eternal life'" (John 4:9-13).

This scripture stood out to me so much because I was thirsty for something and only God could fill the void, and He did. He said if I keep going after things like men, money, and fame, I would get thirsty again and again, but when I come to Him and seek Him, I would never thirst. He will fill every void and the fulfillment only comes from Him.

All of my past sins and regrets about losing my virginity did not matter. He showed me that He was the perfect gift of love and that His love was not based on my behavior. I was putting entirely too much pressure on myself to be perfect and that was not what He was looking for. Once He revealed this to me, whenever I failed, I knew I had to pray. I soon learned that moving past the thoughts of condemnation was a process. Even though I knew about God's perfect love, the thoughts of Him being disappointed in me would still resurface and take my focus off of what I already knew. It was like a tennis match, back and forth with what I knew and what the enemy wanted me to know. I had to constantly remind myself, "He does not love you based on your choices." There is no condemnation for those who are in Christ Jesus (Romans 8:1). I had to fully realize that I could never do enough wrong to get God to stop loving me. His word says that no death or life shall be able to separate us from the love of God (Romans 8:38-39). However, making the choice of losing my virginity did slow me down. There were still consequences for my actions; I just wish I had gotten up faster. I beat myself up for way too long. The best thing to do is to ask for forgiveness and get back up. I placed too much value in my virginity. I did not understand the full value of grace, and trying to do it all in my own strength was just wearing me down. Although I was spending time with Him, I was still focused on the wrong things. I was serving Him out of duty and not devotion, trying to make up for my wrongs. It was a mental battle, but ultimately, I came out stronger.

From then on I started growing in my relationship with Christ more by reading the Word, going to church and asking God for direction with my future. I began thinking that I had sinned so much before that maybe God didn't want me to pursue a career in acting anymore. I even thought to myself that maybe I would have to become a nun. At the time, I still struggled with fully grasping that God loves His children by grace and not by our works so that no man could boast (Ephesians 2:9). I continued to pray and eventually, God revealed to me that I would work with youth and help them overcome obstacles. Questioning this I instantly began thinking how would it be possible for me to do ministry *and* have my dream career at the same time? I honestly didn't think it was possible. A month after college graduation, I still really didn't know which direction that I wanted to go in. I didn't know if I wanted to work with youth in ministry and obey God or continue to pursue my career in the entertainment industry. I had never seen a preacher that I knew really following their creative dreams. And besides, the entertainment industry stressed that you couldn't do anything but focus on pursuing your career. My views and representation on this matter were limited. I didn't think ministry and career could work, so I made a choice to focus just on acting because in my heart, that's what I really wanted to do.

One of my good friends secured an internship at CBS studios in California and it inspired me to seek after jobs there. I mean, I always wanted to be in California anyways, so why not? I ended up applying to a Performing Arts school in Pasadena, California as a Theatre Director. I emailed my resume, and the owner of the studio answered inviting me to California for an in-person interview (this was before Skype, Facetime or Google Hangouts were popular). Since my friend was already there at CBS and she had her own apartment, I had a place to stay once I got there. I flew out to California and had the interview. I was hired on the spot and they gave me $50.00 for taking time and meeting with them. We discussed finding housing, my work hours, and the pay rate was $25.00 an hour. That wasn't bad for a girl coming right out of college in 2007. I was making $50,000.00 a year straight out of school in another state. On top of that, it also happened to be a Christian dance school. Ideally, I could still be doing ministry and entertainment. This was perfect. The owner of the school gave me a week to get back to her with my answer. I went back to Chicago so anxious because first, I had not expected to get the job and second, I was so afraid to move to California all by myself. I wasn't sure that I was mature enough to handle the pressures of the real world because of some of the choices I had made in college. There was still this hole in my heart of not feeling worthy, so I knew that I wasn't ready for that move.

I was mature enough to know that I didn't want a person or an opportunity to fill that void. Despite California being a dream of mine for so many years, I wasn't completely healed from my past mistakes and I didn't want to make choices to fill the void that I could possibly regret later. I knew if I took the job, I would be taking it solely to fill the sense of emptiness that was still inside me. You need character and a solid identity in the industry and I knew I wasn't there yet. I also knew that if I was going to move to California, I wanted to be on television. Working at the theatre did not guarantee that. I gathered my thoughts and came to the conclusion that if I was not going to move to California to be on television, then I might as well stay home. I started thinking bigger and rested in the fact that I could stay in Chicago and create my own theater company where I would still be around my family. Once that was fully established, then I'd come back to California for acting. It was the perfect plan, and plans always go as designed, right?

CHAPTER SIX

Choices

Before I could even move on with my perfect plan, there was still another option in play. Around that time, my church was also in need of a Youth Pastor. So my choices were between taking the job in Pasadena, California making $25.00 an hour, or become the Youth Pastor at my church and teach preschool for free while also working to eventually start my own theatre? I asked so many people for advice especially family and friends. I was scared to be honest with them because I didn't know if I was mature enough to handle the lifestyle of living in California. So I asked Aunti what she thought I should do and she told me to go pray. She would say, "You can't ever lose with God on your side!" So through fear, excitement and uncertainty, I went in my room, got on my knees and prayed. I asked God, what would be the best choice for me? And as I was praying, I opened my bible to the scripture "No one who leaves his family or friends for my sake will fail to receive a hundred times as much in this present age" (Mark 10:29-30). I felt it was confirmation because it said to me that I was sacrificing something that I wanted, for the gospel. So I took the position as the Youth Director at my church and I let go of my dream of moving to California for now. I started working with youth and I created a program called "The Scream Project!" The purpose was to inspire youth to speak out about their issues, instead of being silent and to find their identity in Christ, instead of their pain. This program helped me as well because that's where I discovered the truth about my value and identity. What I was struggling with within myself earlier, I was now able to fully grasp. I understood that my value doesn't come from my parents, my dream coming true or not, or my birthday being the same day as Oprah Winfrey. My value comes from the fact that I am a child of God and that He died on the cross for me and He *chose* me. That no matter what obstacle occurred in my life, nothing had the power to stop the will of God in my life, but me. As I taught the youth to speak over themselves, I began to speak over myself also. *"I am a chosen generation; I am a royal priesthood and my value never changes. I am claimed by the Lord"*. Ironically, *The Scream Project* was a personal breakthrough for me and my identity, and I knew now that my dreams could come true, no matter what.

Therefore, I resigned from being a youth pastor and went back to pursuing my career in acting. It seemed impulsive to everyone but me. I remember Aunti was so upset with me for making that choice. People at the church were even saying that I was using my gift for the devil. But *I* had a dream, and it was something that I was committed to. In my mind, I couldn't see how to execute both ministry work and acting. And therefore, I didn't seek God this time; I just did what I wanted to do.

I had to start building my network and looking for jobs, so I immediately got on my computer and went to Craigslist to start searching for acting jobs day and night. My first job was a short film titled "Escaped!" where I played a victim kidnapped by her husband. Then I auditioned for a community theatre company, Soul Savin Productions. I needed to brush up on my acting skills and working with Soul Savin Production really helped my technique. I also began working at The Black Ensemble Theatre. I started as an intern and, eventually, got a role in the show. I worked at The Harold Washington Cultural Center, with Messiah Equiano Productions as well as LA Holts Productions. I was really building my resume so that I could be more prepared for acting on television and then eventually, once I gained the courage, to move to California.

I was going for my dream with boldness, belief and confidence that I was going to be a star. I was on my way to get that Oscar.

CHAPTER SEVEN

Affirmation

It was 4AM. I was in bed sound asleep when my telephone began to ring. I shot up, fairly surprised and somewhat delirious. I leaned over to the bedside, and picked up the phone. On the other end of the line I heard a lady introduce herself as a nurse. Shortly after, all I heard was, "She's gone." All I could do was barely utter the words "thank you" through my dry swallow, and

I hung up the phone. I took a deep breath and I called my pastor directly after.

"The nurse just called," I said, "She's gone." My Pastor hung up the phone and I immediately jumped out of bed, got in the car, and rushed over to the hospital to see Aunti one last time. I was devastated. Aunti suffered from a ruptured aneurysm. *"What were we going to do now?"* was the main thought running through my head. My security blanket, my protector, my guide and my affirmation, was gone. This was not only a huge loss for me, but it was a huge loss for my family, our church, and my community in general. Aunti, Doris Stewart, was my **mother, mom,** and the backbone of our family. She was the matriarch; she took care of everyone. She was our hero, the rescuer, and our strength. When everyone had problems in our family, she was the person they called on and she was the one to solve them, and now she was gone.

My mother was a special lady, one of a kind. She adopted my brother, my sister, and me as a single parent and as a dialysis patient for twenty-two years. She was on dialysis due to kidney failure and had to use medicine at home four times daily, but you would never know. She never allowed her sickness to stop her from living life. She loved to cook, clean with bleach (haha), and wear the biggest and most colorful hats to church. She loved perfume, Italian food and most of all, prayer. Every weekend at our house, there was a prayer service, and every day, she found a way to give us a sermon at home. Her favorite sermons to direct towards me were "Shakila, don't step out of this house looking like a supermodel and your room looking like a hog pen!" Or, "Shakila, I'm tired of these boys scratching at my door, you better not bring no babies in this house!" She sacrificed so much for my siblings and me. Even until the last week of her life, she still was guiding us. She was truly one of a kind. The average dialysis patient only lived ten years, but because of her faith in Jesus, she doubled that. I will always remember one piece of advice my mother gave me in the hospital just a week before she passed. I was sitting there with her talking about life, when she interrupted me by grabbing my hand and said, "Shakila, you know you have to let me go, but I will always be with you because you know the Lord. Now take care of your brother and sister and know there ain't no purpose of living life if you ain't gonna have no joy." That moment hit me so hard, because before, I hadn't fully realized that I would have to let her go. I remember leaving the hospital and calling all of her friends telling them to please make sure they go see her, because after having that conversation with her, I knew that I had to let her go.

At times, I never knew if my mom was proud of me or not. But while I would go visit and spend the night while she was in the hospital, every single time I would walk in the room, her eyes would light up. It was like she felt safe. She was always so happy to see me when I walked in the room. Mom had a lot of respect for me; she knew that I could handle whatever life threw my way even when I thought I could not. It was like she was saying, "YOU GOT THIS!" and boy did I need that affirmation because immediately after her passing, my entire life transformed. I became a full adult at the age of twenty-six. If I am being completely honest, most of my life, I was self-centered, career focused and very spoiled. Now, I had to plan a funeral, become head of the household, and adopt my ten-year-old brother. I didn't have a job or money, and I had no idea how to be a parent. I was terrified because I had no idea how we were going to survive. I had been so focused on my dream that I hadn't stopped to consider alternative avenues. It was a drastic change going from an artist, to raising kids. It was not easy, but because I saw my mom do it, I believed that I could do it too. It was definitely extremely overwhelming at times. I could not fully grieve mom's passing because I had to make sure that my siblings were okay. I had to make sure that the bills were paid and that we were safe. I had to take care of the house, get the groceries, take them to counseling and attend basketball games. I had to live like the most unimaginable thing was not happening to my family.

But God was so faithful. Whenever I missed her, I would dream that we were at the park laughing and eating, and she would kiss me on my forehead. I would wake up and feel so much better. One night, I felt so overwhelmed with all the responsibilities of raising a family and she came to me in a dream. In this one, she prayed for me and encouraged me so I could make it through my hardships.

During this time, I was dating a guy who proposed to me and I didn't know what to say and so I prayed that my mother would give me an answer. In my dream she said, "I can't make that choice for you. This is a choice that you'll have to make!" Then I woke up. I made the choice not to get married. I felt that I wasn't ready. These dreams were such a comforting experience because I knew, without a doubt, that God and my mother were watching after me.

Life Coach:

I needed direction more than ever now, since mom was gone. I prayed continually, got a life coach and, with the support of family and friends, I felt that God was telling me that it was time to start my performing arts company, so I did. I took on the mindset that all of my life obstacles were working as my strength, so I would build on them.

I called my theatre company, Shakila's Dream Shop Performing Arts Company, Inspiring You To Dream, Believe and Succeed. I started teaching youth musical theatre classes. I was directing so many youth musicals and everything was going amazingly well. I began to travel and teach acting, dance and modeling classes. I was finally getting my footing while walking this new path of being a parent and having a part of my dream. Then God gave me the idea for a character named "Dreamah!" Dreamah is an animated character inspired by my life story of being adopted, yet having a positive outlook on life. I later decided to change my company's name to Dreamah Studios Inc.!

Despite my mother passing, over the next couple of years my siblings and I did well. Through this experience, I realized that there are so many obstacles that women are forced to conquer, and because of this, many sacrifice their dreams and stop dreaming altogether. I thought, "Why don't we conquer our dreams and make them a reality?" And because I'm creative, I decided I wanted to start a movement that would push women to go after their dreams, so I created a workshop called, Walk This Way Movement. I gathered ten of my friends together and told them my idea. We put together a video; I directed it, sent out a press release and had a launch event. Our second class was shot on Windy City Live! I was so excited because my company, a program that I created was on TV, and the women loved it! It was a huge deal in Chicago. Two months later, I was on an *Ask Steve* segment for the Steve Harvey Show and later, Dr. Oz. My siblings and I were overcoming and pushing through! My brother was on his way to college with a scholarship for track and field, my sister was marrying her high school sweetheart and I was finally feeling like my dream was coming back.

Though I was walking in my purpose, soon enough, I was going to experience the realities and responsibilities that come along with being a business owner. Although God gave me the vision and I was becoming so successful and had so much favor, I was learning the reality of being a businesswoman. No matter how well your business is doing, you can't quit your day job unless you have the finances in your hand or bank account. To pay your bills with uncommitted contracts, you need to have money saved. I had quit teaching at the schools, which was my primary source of income. I had fallen into a complete financial hole. I made the choice to stop working because I just knew that I was going to get a break in business through Walk This Way Movement, but I did not. In order to get back on my feet, I started taking business classes, applying for grants, and networking. I began dating a wonderful man. Without asking, he rescued me financially and emotionally. He truly had my back and took great care of me. He helped to fill this void in my heart of losing my mom and that was what I really needed.

He and I met on January 3, 2015 at my cousin's birthday party; we immediately hit it off. I remember he was a very well dressed man from head to toe, very sharp. You could tell by the way he dressed and carried himself that he was a man of means. He was very sweet to me; we went on trips, and he bought me designer purses, heels, and clothes. He would surprise me with roses, cook dinner for me, if I had a toothache he would run to make sure that I had medicine, and most importantly, he was one of the first people close to me to ask me how I felt after my mother's death. Being with him was freedom for me because he took care of me and I had been use to taking care of everyone else and running my business. He was very sweet and affectionate, just an overall very loving guy. When I was having financial issues in my company, he helped me out so much. For my birthday, he got me a pair of diamond earrings and a diamond necklace with a beautiful custom-made cake with high heels. He was so special to me, but the only issue was that I felt was compromising my relationship with God. I began spending nights with him and not going to church as much. I told myself it didn't matter much because things were looking up for me. Everything was going so well. I was networking hard and working on a contract with a large company when all of a sudden God said, "It's time to go to California!"

I was like, *"No God! Not now! Things are finally coming together in my business; I'm dating a great guy. Nooo, not now!"* I knew that by moving to California I wouldn't be able to continue my relationship, and that I would have to let him go. That was hard because he was such a source of strength and support for me. I was scared to move to California without that safety net and risk struggling. I knew he wasn't going to move with me, but, when God says you have to go, you have to go and walk the path He lays out for you. I needed to pray. I needed my life coach and support from family and friends to make that choice. My boyfriend was supportive, but he did not like it. I knew that God would not just tell anyone to go to California because California doesn't have the best reputation. If God was telling me to go, I was quite curious, and I had to see what lay ahead. This was not just my dream, this was my purpose; I knew there was a deeper and even more meaningful reason for me to go. I remembered the words of my mom "You can never go wrong with following the Lord!"

CHAPTER EIGHT

Abraham Faith

Leaving Chicago was an internal struggle because I knew that if I moved to California, not only were my boyfriend and I going to break up, once I moved I'd have to start all over with my business making new connections. I didn't have any financial security in California. It was so hard to tell my boyfriend that I was officially leaving, but he understood because he always knew that it was a dream of mine. I was determined to obey God, but it still hurt both of us badly. A lot of women tend to choose their relationship over their dreams; I was blessed enough to have a support system around me pushing me towards mine.

I remember my best friend calling me saying, "Shakila, I feel like it is time for you to move to California." Next, my life coach called me saying the same thing a few weeks later. Everywhere I went, people kept bringing up me moving to California. Then, one day when I was in the shower, (Jesus always talks to me while I'm in the shower; I guess because I'm most quiet and able to listen in there) He said, "You are worth following your dreams Shakila. It's okay to do something for yourself." After that, I cried because I knew everything was about to change and that I would have to tell my boyfriend and really start planning.

Although it was a hard choice, once I made up my mind, it was over. I was committed to obeying God and moving to California to fulfill this fifteen-year dream of mine. I worked the entire summer to save money, and any job I could get, I was doing. From selling coffee to working parades, to working at the airport, I was everywhere.

I had only four months to prepare and save enough money to move to California. I had accountability partners, my life coach, my best friend and prayer as confirmation, so with that, I sold all of my furniture. People thought I was crazy. They would say things like, "You're too old to be chasing a childhood dream, and don't you want to get married?" Others were happy for me, but getting through it was truly a process. I was so nervous, but I trusted God and if He said I should go, I had to. In retrospect, if I didn't come here I wouldn't be writing this book. I was too comfortable in Chicago and God needed me to get away and be by myself so that He could really have my full attention without any distractions. He still would have blessed me had I stayed in Chicago, but now it was going to be even greater because I obeyed Him. Though not without heartache, it seemed like the timing was right as well. My sister was getting married in April, my brother was going to college in August and my lease on my condo was up in September. Everything was lining up and Mom would have been so proud of her children. I know that she was in heaven smiling and fighting for us.

I went out for dinners and partied with family and special friends from my childhood before I left. I knew I had no connections or anything in California. Fortunately, my life coach and spiritual mother kept telling me, "God says you have to have 'Abraham Faith'!" I took this seriously, and I knew that I needed faith to move. In order to build my faith, I had to consistently read Genesis 12, "Now the LORD had said to Abram: 'Get out of your country, from your family and from your father's house, to a land that I will show you. I will make you a great nation; I will bless you and make your name great; and you shall be a blessing. I will bless those who bless you, and I will curse him who curses you; and in you all the families of the earth shall be blessed'" (Genesis 12:1-3).

I just knew it was going to be undeniably difficult to move so far away, especially alone. I had to leave everything that I knew: my siblings, friends, business opportunities, and connections. Out of everything, the most difficult to leave would be my brother and sister. They were my everything. I knew I was going to miss them so much.

Nevertheless, I had to put my trust in God and believe that He was going to provide for me in this new environment and on this journey. This was absolutely terrifying, but I had to do it. This was a *chin up, shoulders back* moment for me. However, through this whole process of moving, I learned that God will never leave or forsake you and He will always send help and honor your obedience. Though my boyfriend was hurt about the move, I had to obey God if I wanted peace of mind. I had to plan many aspects of my move. I especially needed to work out where I was going to live and work. Although it was a dream of mine to finally move to California, it seemed as if I was taking several steps backward.

Order my steps Lord:

Initially, I thought I had everything planned out. My plan was to stay on a friend's couch until I found an apartment. I had my car shipped from Chicago to Los Angeles, and on September 27, 2017, with $300.00 in my pocket, I grabbed my suitcase and boarded the American Airlines plane. With my natural hair in two French braids, I knew this was a walk of faith; I never wear my natural hair! I am a Diva. I always have a sew-in or finger waves, but I was on a journey. I managed to secure an internship at a prominent dance studio in hopes that after the internship ended, I would secure a full-time position there. Also, a promotional job that I worked for in Chicago transferred to California, so things were lining up.

CHAPTER NINE

Chin Up

Moving to California as a thirty-three-year-old adult was very interesting because I was starting over and leaving everything behind that I knew. The whole environment and everything was completely different. Once I arrived, my stomach turned and I immediately became home sick. I did not immediately realize it, but I was going through a grieving process. Not having anyone

63

physically there was taking a toll on me. It was a lot for me to leave my boyfriend because he was such a huge support for me, emotionally. I didn't have someone to hug and kiss me or hold me through disappointments when things were hard. In Chicago, I could go to him and get a hug, or better yet, go to my sister's house if I was hungry, or needed a laugh. I could go to my friends' homes if I needed anything. My safety net, my tribe, was gone. I was here alone. It's hard when you don't have community while going after your dreams. The pressure was on me from back home to come to Los Angeles, become successful and gain an acting contract. Television makes things look so easy, but the reality was that it was extremely difficult, especially without any money or direction.

I didn't know that I was grieving my family until one night after bible study, I went home and it suddenly hit me. I was like *"Jesus, what did I do? I left my man for this??"* Haha. I was listening to all kind of sad music: the Whispers, and the Temptations lol. I was doing the most. But at the end of the day, I knew that if I wanted to get towards my destiny, I had to walk it out. I had to go through the process because going home was not an option and I had to trust God. Moving to California was *my* dream, this was what I always wanted, but it didn't look like how I pictured it.

I had a distant cousin who lived in my new city and I asked him if I could stay with him for at least one month to get used to living here and save some extra rent money before I moved in with roommates. My job transfer from Chicago went from $18.00 and hour to $14.00 an hour. Talk about a setback. I was so excited that the job was transferrable that I didn't check to see if the pay rate was the same, which I guess was a mistake I made due to my optimism. I was too busy trying to figure everything out. Alongside this, I had to pay $30.00 every day to park for my job. So with that job I was making about $6.00 an hour. I thought to myself, this could not have been the path God chose for me. Then, a couple days before I was about to start the internship, I called the Dance Studio and the director told me that the internship was no longer available because they had to give it to a college student. I was so devastated. Getting the internship at the studio was one of the main reasons why I came to California. Now I had no job, no money, and I had to move out of my cousin's house and in with roommates sleeping on the sofa. I really wanted to go home this time. All these thoughts were going through my head, *"Why did I leave Chicago? I used to live in a two bedroom, two-bath condo, complete with a fireplace, a Jacuzzi, and I ran a business. What was my life coming to?"*

I would listen to a lot of TD Jakes' sermons; I would call the Christian network TBN for prayer, and call my good friends for both prayer and guidance. It was really hard and humbling at the same time because the people around me were all established, so my family and friends from Chicago thought things were easy. Yet, for me, I was still heavily grieving my mom, my boyfriend, my siblings, and my old place. I wasn't focused and I knew that I wasn't making any progress. It was a lot to detach myself from. I was so used to having the responsibility of caring for others; now I was on my own and that was something I had to get used to. I was an "empty-nester"; I was like a mom whose kids gone off to college and now she could start living for herself, but had to learn how.

Through it all, my heart said, "You can't just go home", so I humbled myself once again. I decided to call the studio asking, "Do you need any volunteers? If so, I am willing!" I remembered God's word says, "If you are willing and obedient, you shall eat the good of the land" (Isaiah 1:19).

I am totally glad I humbled myself by volunteering. Because of this, I was able to meet the legendary Berry Gordy, the founder and creator of Motown records and creator of The Wiz. Outside of him being such a legend, I had directed the Wiz musical when I was in Chicago, so this was a very special moment for me. I realized then, and remind myself now, that volunteering can get you through the door sometimes. Despite the early setbacks, I was still chasing my dreams. And I learned that humility brings honor. I was tested to see if I would go back home and I passed.

I didn't give up. I prayed and cried, read the bible, and starting going to Oasis LA church. I went to Growth Track, an inner healing class called Freedom, and I joined an entrepreneurship program all at the church. I also got involved working with the youth there and they even asked me to start preaching sermons. Oasis was where I felt safe and is where I found my new church family.

CHAPTER TEN

Favor

God showed me so much favor. There were so many miraculous and significant things that happened to me in the next six weeks of living in California; I just couldn't believe it.

While volunteering at the Dance studio, I ended up assisting the sister of one of Hollywood's top writer's. This was amazing for me, and even more amazing was I knew I was

68

working hard for it, as if I was actually going to get a check. But God was not concerned with giving me a load of money at this point, He was helping me build and develop my character. **Character will get you into doors that your talent cannot.** Therefore, while the production was going on, I had front row seats next to all these celebrities I knew and admired. I also learned how to direct theatre productions on another level. Sometimes, it's about building and nurturing relationships with people and not about what you get to take from another person. When you are working your way up, it is sometimes good to volunteer just so you can build these relationships.

Later, I volunteered at another event and met the Chief Executive Officer of a prominent movie studio in LA. It was a huge studio that has been around for many years, and I was at the table with so many prominent leaders in the entertainment industry including Netflix, Nickelodeon, Viacom, BET, and VH1. I was garnering so much information about the industry that I would need to know for my career in acting. I thank God that He allowed me to sit at the table with all these great men and women. I learned, through experience, **when you humble yourself, great things follow**.

I marveled, "Wow, God. I get it. You are showing me that I am meant to be here." God was showing out and because of my desire to be on television, I was going to all of the television shows I possibly could go to. There was one that was particularly momentous, because Steve Harvey had moved his show from Chicago to California the same time I had moved. I knew that there was something significant about this, and that there would be a possible connection there. Back in Chicago, I had been on a segment of the Steve Harvey Show called "Ask Steve" and at the end of my segment he says, "Ladies and gentlemen welcome the newest member of the Harvey family, Shakila Harvey!" It was such a fun episode. So this time being in California, I reminded him of who I was, and that I was in the audience, and he remembered.

To me this was another sign. I knew that I was getting closer to my dream; thank you, Jesus! So, I'm on his show in California and Steve plays this game called, "Harvey's Hundreds" where I had to pick a number and find the match, similar to the game, Mary Maid. The producers called me down from the audience and Steve asked me, "What do you need this money for?" I replied, "I need a security deposit for my new apartment" (even though I didn't have an apartment yet, I definitely needed it). I played the matching game live on national television with my hair still in those two French braids. Ironically, I had the same dress on that I did when I was on his show the first time in Chicago. However, Steve started helping me find answers. The last match was the word "California" and Steve assisted me in getting it. What I said was, "California, I'm here!" It was symbolic to me that California was the winning answer.

Steve asked me a series of questions, like "What are you here for?" and "What do you need?" I told him, "I'm here for acting and I want to be on a sitcom." He looked at me for a minute, deadly silent, and said, "I know someone…", but then the producers came and walked me back to my seat. They interrupted our entire meeting, but I got to walk away with $500 that day. They cut me the check the same day, which was great because I really needed it. God was faithful to His word and He was providing for me.

Be kind:

A woman of my word, The Diva in me was getting crushed. The following week, I had tickets to The Real talk show; I really was going to every show! I remember talking to my cousin who asked, "Do you want to be a talk show host or something? What's going on with you?" The downside to going to The Real that morning was that in order to get there on time, I had to be up at 4:30AM. I honestly did not really want to go, but I said I was going to, and I'm a woman of my word. Even though I invited two other friends to go with me, they didn't come. It was obviously too early for them, too. That day, the audience on The Real won a $100 gift card to a jewelry store. This really excited me; it was worth getting up for after all. Thank you, The Real! But what happened after I stepped out of The Real parking lot was one of the most significant things in my life. Talk about God ordering your steps.

I was walking out and this short, beautiful Caucasian lady wearing a cute pink blazer and blue jeans asked me, "Do you know where the Warner Brothers studio is located?" "No," I replied. "But maybe it's over that way." Although I didn't know, I tried to be as helpful as I possibly could. I was being kind. The lady had two other women with her; they were so cute and they called themselves The Golden Girls. They were all vacationing from Pennsylvania. The lady in the pink blazer then asked me a question, "What do you have planned for today?"

"Nothing, I'm going home." I responded. Because I had to get up so early that morning, I didn't really care what I looked like. I was wearing a pink top, light blue jeans, a black and white sweater with black heels, and my hair was still in two French braids. I may not have looked my cutest, but hey, at least I was there! (Sometimes you have to stop worrying about being cute and just go). The lady in the pink blazer proceeded to ask, "We have an extra VIP ticket to the Ellen Show, would you like to come with us? Our cousin was supposed to come, but she didn't show up." I was amazed. I had just met these people and they were inviting me to go do something that I really always wanted to do.

"Oh my gosh, yes please", I responded. "Let me email the producer to see if you could you get in", she replied. I didn't have much hope. I was doubtful that the producer was going to answer; they'd clearly be too busy working on other things. However, to my surprise, the producer responded in thirty seconds with a "yes". I couldn't believe it; I was going to be in the audience of The Ellen Show! Clearly, getting up at 4:30AM and bumping into three Caucasian ladies was great for me! They then invited me to breakfast since the show did not start until 1:00PM. The lady in the pink blazer said, "It's on us. We have husbands that take care of us." I later learned that these three women had been trying to get tickets to this show for six years. This was yet another sign for me that if God sends you to a place, He will provide for you. He will supply you with all your needs. He will send people to help you along the way, if you are obedient to Him.

These ladies were very special. One of them told me that she had a dream the night before that a stranger came with them to the show, and that stranger ended up being me. I knew it was God. When we got to the show, I learned that it was Ellen's 15th year anniversary show, so she surprised the audience with a trip to Vegas. She also gave us another ticket to come back to her 15 Days of Christmas show. God was really showing out and I was outdone! I have no idea why He favors me, but I know He loves me so much. That morning, I left home at 4:30AM and mad. I came back home that evening with a trip to Vegas, new friends, and a ticket to the Holiday Show. That night the Golden Girls and I went to In-n-Out burger before I dropped them off at their hotel. They gave me their numbers and $30.00 for gas. If this story doesn't make you believe in God, I don't know what will. These ladies were complete strangers in my life, but the Golden

Girls and I began to talk every other day until we went to the show again.

The second time on the Ellen Show:

At the second show, I met the Golden Girls at Marshalls. I was a little frustrated because I didn't have enough time to do my nails. I literally had the red nail polish on the passenger seat in my car ready to polish them while we drove, when one of them said to me, "We're going to get our nails done. You can't go on television without your nails done!"

This really made me think of the passage from Proverbs 10:22, which says, "The blessings of the Lord will make you rich and add no sorrow to it." When God blesses you with something, He makes it easy. I didn't have to compromise my integrity and there were no strings attached. On the holiday show, we won another trip to Vegas, a $500 gift card for Uber Eats, a $300 gift card to Home Depot, a $1200 mattress, a $500 coffee pot, a $500 gift card for Ellen's royal china, and a home security camera. This really was absolutely amazing. *"Thank you, God, you just secured me a housewarming party*, and Ellen just blessed me with so much I would need for my apartment that I didn't even have yet"*. Once again, it reminded me of Mark 10:28-30, "Then

Peter began to say to Him, 'See, we have left all and followed You.' So Jesus answered and said, 'Assuredly, I say to you, there is no one who has left their house or brothers or sisters or father or mother or wife or children or lands, for My sake and the gospel's, who shall not receive a hundredfold now in this time-- houses and brothers and sisters and mothers and children and lands, with persecutions--and in the age to come, eternal life.'" God knew that it was hard for me to leave my family, but He just continued to bless me and give me winks along the way. ***Is God telling you to let go of something or someone that you are afraid to? Do it! He will back you up.*** It's hard, but you can do all things through Christ, who strengthens you (Philippians 4:13).

After the show, the Golden Girls and I went to a famous steak house here in LA. We took several pictures and promised to stay in touch with each other. And guess what? We still do! God brought us together for a reason and I'm always excited to see how everything comes together. It pays to be kind. On that early morning, I merely stopped and gave them directions and that turned into a friendship of a lifetime.

The blessings continued to flow:

Everything was going great. Late one evening, I received a call from a friend. She said, "I have box office tickets to a Lakers' game. Are you free?" It didn't take me long to reply, "Yes!" I was wondering how on earth I was able to get free tickets to a Lakers Game in the Box Office. I asked God about what I did to deserve this. Do you know what His reply to me was? "You're my daughter and I want you to experience the best. No man or woman can bless you like I can. I am Jehovah Jireh—your provider—and I want to be that in your life." Ladies, if God wants to be your provider, let Him be it!

Taking Risks:

I was finally getting used to California and I was feeling secure and confident. I wanted to host a Walk This Way Movement class, and I wanted one of the speakers to be from the show, Insecure. I reached out to her personal assistant (I don't remember how I got her information but, if you know me, you know I mix prayer with research, and I always find what I'm looking for). I sent an email out to the personal assistant to tell her about myself and the Walk This Way Movement. Admittedly, I was nervous to send the email, but with God on my side, I sent it anyway. I was so excited; I called one of my friends to tell her about everything. Her reply was perfect, "Girl, you got this. Go for it." Then we prayed together.

Shortly after the phone call, to my surprise, the personal assistant replied to my email. She wrote that, although she was busy during that time, she would let me know if something came up, because you never know. I was so grateful that she responded.

Then, the same friend that prayed with me over the phone saw an advertisement online that the same actress I wanted to get involved in the Walk This Way Movement Inc. was speaking at an event in LA. What was even better was that the event was FREE! My thanks go to God. Here we go again! I knew that, if only I could meet this actress, I could get her to speak at my event. I ended up meeting her and handed her my card. She was such a beautiful soul for the Kingdom of God and she promised me that she'd reach out after her tour. ***What I learned here was that God is faithful when we make a move. He will always back you up.***

The same night I met the actress, I ended up meeting six ladies, and I shared my story with them. Not long afterwards, inside the parking lot of the mall, we prayed and went on a fast together. Once again, talk about God ordering your steps! What

God did for me within the first six weeks of living in California was the most accelerated I've ever seen Him move in my life. I ended up getting a job working at a promotional company and I got tickets to the Nickelodeon Kids Choice Awards, Iheart Radio Awards, Jay Z's concert, Bruno Mars, Ascap Awards and an awards show honoring Nipsey Hussle and Kash Doll. God showed me so much favor. When God says that He will exceed all that we could ever think or imagine, believe Him (Ephesians 3:20).

CHAPTER ELEVEN

You Got This

As we all know, all things come to an end, and unfortunately that includes the fun things. Suddenly, a shift happened. It was a real turning point in my life. I was no longer humbling myself and that was when I found myself in the midst of a humbling situation. My reality was, I was sleeping on a friend's couch with no consistent income, and no real plan. I thought that volunteering at the Dance Studio would get me a job and it did not. I had no other choice but to get a real job paying only $12.00 an hour.

I had to be off my friend's couch by January 15th and I was beyond stressed because the housing situation in California is way more expensive than Chicago and I did not have the money. All I could think about was Abraham Faith. I meditated on this scripture daily, praying that I would find an apartment in my price range before my deadline. I was reminded that Sarah and Abraham were too old to have a baby, but God promised them that they would have one despite their old age. I needed an apartment and I didn't have much by way of finances, but I needed a miracle as big as the one God promised to Abraham and Sarah (Genesis 15:2-6). True to form, the Lord fulfilled His promise in Genesis 21:1-2, "The Lord kept his word and did for Sarah exactly what he had promised. She became pregnant, and she gave birth to a son for Abraham in his old age".

I meditated on this scripture day and night praying that I would find an apartment before my deadline because it was an impossible situation, similar to Abraham and Sarah's. For three months, I was visiting houses, reaching out to landlords, and sending emails. It was a strenuous process. Some of the apartments in my price range were as small as a closet door. No joke. Some of them didn't even have a stove or refrigerator. Artists in LA live a very humbling life before they make it big, and it's rare to live in a place without roommates. In LA, it costs about $1300.00 a month for a studio. In Chicago, my rent was $1250.00 for a two bedroom and two bathrooms! Regardless of the odds, you should know by now that God always comes through.

One day I'm on the couch when out of nowhere I am surfing the internet; next I realize, I am calling a number I had previously called, and the landlord approved the amount I could afford. I was so relieved; there were eighty people in line to get this place and I was the one who got it! On January 5th, I found the apartment I needed ten days before I had to move out of my friend's house. I told you, God is faithful.

This apartment was beautiful. It had a new refrigerator, a stove, and it was a studio in East Hollywood. Who would have thought my first ever apartment in California would be in Hollywood?! Well, I know God knew. In the mornings, when I woke up, I would get up and look out the window at the palm trees and beyond them at the hills where the famous HOLLYWOOD sign sits. It was like a dream, and a dream come true. My next challenge was to find $2,575 for a security deposit. I did the research and God did me another favor. I was able to get a company to pay the security deposit for me. Wow! God was blessing me, again, with yet another miracle, proving to me that He was my provider. He was never going to leave me, nor was He going to forsake me. He helped me so much in this transition.

CHAPTER TWELVE

Walk This Way

Finally, in my apartment, I felt a bit more settled. I would go hiking once a week to Beachwood Canyon so I could talk to God to get clarity, direction, and peace. One day while hiking, I started crying. I had to seek God for direction, and He kept telling me to keep my Abraham Faith. He told me that I was on an accelerated path to my destiny. I kept asking Him, "How?"

because nothing in my life situation was adding up to me being on this accelerated path. What was going on with my dreams? I was not making progress. I know God was blessing me with so much, but I still had no job and no steady income. I did not feel secure. I moved from all my family, and these promises that were made were not adding up or coming together. I felt so defeated. I boldly asked, "God, why aren't things moving like You said that they would?" He replied clearly, "Because you haven't surrendered to the call of ministry over your life." I was like, *"Really?"* I was so shocked. I couldn't believe that was the answer. It didn't make any sense. How was ministry going to lead me towards a career in acting? I thought to myself, "I could have done ministry in Chicago. I could have stayed with my man!" But I now understand that it was the truth only God could reveal. I continued to pray and God said, "How can you expect me to move like I want to in this life if you're not inviting me or my plan into it? You're trying to do it your way Shakila, and it isn't going to work because you don't know where you're going!"

My mouth dropped. I was like, "Really, God? Could you not have told me this in Chicago?" Oh, now I see how much of a smart mouth I was being with God. Thankfully, God is a loving father; He understands where you are coming from. I learned that if I was going to believe that God was going to do something, then I had to be open to doing it His way. Since I was walking by faith and faith alone, I had no idea where I was going. I had to let go of what I thought my California Dream was going to be and receive what God wanted it to be, and that wasn't easy. However, that was the only way that I was going get the promise God had for me. I had asked God, "So you're telling me... I waited fifteen years to come to California to be on television acting and *You* said that I was on an accelerated path, and now You're saying ministry? You want me to lay down my dreams and pursue ministry?"

I was reminded of another passage. "Take your son, your only son—yes, Isaac, whom you love so much—and go to the land of Moriah. Go and sacrifice him as a burnt offering on one of the mountains, which I will show you." (Genesis 22:2)

Let me take a second to get this straight; God had Abraham wait all these years for a son, then He wanted him to sacrifice him. Really God? This is too much. However, Abraham was so committed to God and Genesis 22:3 says, "The next morning Abraham got up early. He saddled his donkey and took two of his servants with him, along with his son, Isaac."

Abraham obeyed God extremely fast. That is because He had a relationship with God, and he trusted Him. So I took this idea on. I laid down my career, let go of what it was I wanted, and said, "God I surrender to Your plan for my life. I let go of what I want for what You want for my life!"

I had to humble myself and surrender my life to Christ; that process consisted of me spending more time praying, fasting, reading the Bible, and going to church. I had to completely change my lifestyle. It wasn't easy, but I was determined to get a clear answer from the Lord on where my life was headed. It was such a hard process for me that I set up a private meeting with a couple at my church who had similar stories about moving to California and having to lay down their dream. I asked them, "What am I getting into? How did you surrender your dream, something that you have been waiting to manifest forever?" This couple talked with me and prayed for me, and I felt peace. If you're struggling to surrender to God, it is okay to reach out to council for help. It is a process. As you can read in Proverbs 11:14, "Where there is no guidance the people fall, but in an abundance of counselors there is victory." In other words, reach out for help! Your destiny depends on it. Reach out to someone who you can trust.

God was ready to do a new thing in my life, but I had to let go of the old to get to the new. Anytime God is doing something new in your life, it will never go the way you expected it to go. Because you are in new and unfamiliar territory, you could never have known you were literally going to *"Walk That Way."* But when you do, you must completely cling to it, and completely trust God. Like in the example of Abraham, God has to become your best friend. Psalm 16:11 says, "You will make known to me the path of life; in your presence is the fullness of joy at your right hand are pleasures forevermore." Whatever we need is in Christ; He will fill every void in your life through spending time in His presence.

Surrendering my life to the Lord has been one of the most amazing times in my life. I promise you, God has literally fulfilled His promise to me and it all came from my relationship with Him being the most important thing—because that's where your life fulfillment will come from, not your career or marriage, looks or bank account, and not even your children. Psalms 34:8 says "Oh taste and see that the Lord is good." Psalm 145:16 says, "He satisfies the desire of every living thing."

"Walking This Way" will require you to let go of old habits, and things that you may have thought were simple. God

may say, let it go. Because it is going to stop you from getting to where He's trying to take you. Remember, God wants you to prosper. He says, "If you are willing and obedient you shall eat the good of the land" (Isaiah 1:19). Talk about obedience. Although surrendering what I wanted for what God wanted was hard for me, it has been one of the most fulfilling things in my life. I cannot stress that enough.

Obedience is better than Sacrifice:

This new lifestyle of surrendering my life was a lot. I woke up one morning, got out of bed and decided to complain about everything: my studio apartment, my job, everything. I had to ask myself, "Why am I complaining so much to God?" I'm telling you that God literally became my best friend. I was literally asking Him everything. Now I'm finally in the place that I dreamt about for the past fifteen years. What has gone wrong? God was telling me "I can't move into your life the way that I want to because your heart is still in Chicago and I need you here!" I was like "Really God? Who am I?"

All these things I was trying to hold on to, God told me to let go of. He told me to leave my family and friends, to follow Him and let Him lead me. It was hard to enjoy these moments because my heart was still in Chicago. It's hard to let go of attachments that you are connected to, especially relationships, but if God says that you must let them go, you must let them go. I wanted to be in a relationship with my boyfriend in Chicago, but I had to let him go.

What I learned from this process of following your dreams was that there are going to be some relationships that you're going to have to let go of, because it's a cost to be the boss, and not everyone wants to pay the cost. The cost is humility, sacrifice and resting in God's promises. You must surrender your own plans for God's plans. You have to let go of the good to get to the great, and letting go of the great allows you to get the best. Girl, God wants you to have the very best! It's a process, but you can do all things through Christ, which strengthens you (Philippians 4:13). It may seem lonely, at first, but you will make it through. You just have to follow Christ and be open to building new relationships for where God is trying to take you. Your destiny is worth it. Your relationships will determine your destiny. Believe that. You want people who are going to push you to live your God-given purpose and not settle, even when you want to give up.

When I first moved to California, one of my friends that I hadn't talked to in years, called me. She was very encouraging. She said, "God wants to present you to the world in a different way. I know that you love to act, model and you're a diva, but God is doing something bigger with your life; I can see you helping youth in foster care." When she said this, I was like, "Girl, bye. I'm not on that." But that did not stop my friend from pushing me. As it is written in Proverbs 27:17, "As iron sharpens iron, so one person sharpens another." Your relationships are very important factors as they relate to your destiny. They say you are the sum of the five people you hang around with the most. Who can you count on your fingers that you hang with?

Holding on Tight:

I can't tell you surrendering and letting go of my dream was easy; it was one of the hardest, scariest processes I've ever been through. My whole life, my core goal was to end generational curses and because I am very strong willed, I was committed to this dream as you can see from my childhood. Acting, modeling and performing were my everything, so, to just let them go, was more than difficult. Fasting, praying, going to church, and building new relationships were all well and good, but I was still holding on to my dream. I still had some humbling to do and some things to let go of. I was a Diva! But being a Diva wasn't going to get me to my destiny. Proverbs 3:12 says, "For the Lord corrects those He loves, as a father corrects a child in whom He delights in."

God loved me so much and He wants success in my life just as much as I do. He was tearing down things in my life that didn't bear fruit, things that were hindering my progress. If I have never heard a plot twist in my life, this one will go down in history as one of the best. I was praying and writing in my journal and just when I thought that I had completely surrendered, God said, "You know that you didn't overcome these obstacles walking in heels right?!" I hollered at this! I laughed so hard because only God could tell me that. The Walk This Way Movement mission statement was, "Teaching women how to overcome obstacles through the art of *walking in heels*!" Ha!

Now it was all making sense. I had to humble myself to get the revelation that I didn't overcome these obstacles in my life being a diva walking in heels. I overcame being in foster care, being adopted, losing my parents, and adopting my siblings, only through the love of Christ, and I had been leaving Him out of the story. I was a leading woman down the wrong path telling them that they were going to overcome their obstacles through "walking in heels!" Don't get me wrong, wearing heels does give you a certain amount of confidence, but that's not how I overcame obstacles and discovering this truth helped me personally and professionally. I didn't want to boast about me being a Christian, but that is a huge part of who I am and that's why I wasn't seeing breakthrough in my business. I was hiding who I really was.

It may seem harsh, but when you're following Christ and you get close to him, He begins to reveal His truth. As John 4:24 says, "God is spirit and we must worship him in spirit and in truth." God wanted my relationship with Him to be completely honest and true. He was being truthful with me. I asked Him for an answer, and He gave it to me. No one else could speak this truth like He did or else I would have taken offense. His correction was direction; His correction was peace, provision, and the best I could possibly receive. He was teaching me that true fulfillment comes from Him. He wanted me to be who He created me to be.

I AM ENOUGH! I AM WHOLE! I AM REAL! This is God's word. He didn't just want me to know, but He wanted me to be confident that He had a plan for my life, and I didn't have to suck up or compromise to get this plan. Everything that I needed was already inside of me. 2 Timothy 2:21 says, "So if anyone purifies himself from anything that is dishonorable, he will be a special instrument. Set apart, useful to the Master, prepared for every good work." I did what I had to do. I let go of behaviors, relationships, and my mindset in order to grow up. His word says, "Humility brings honor." In Proverbs 29:23, it says, "Pride ends in humiliation, while humility brings honor." So, I have realized that humility is my potion to living my best life.

I had to surrender my plans to God and always ask God the scripture to back up what He was telling me. "So God, if I'm not here to act right now, what is the assignment that you have for me?"

Assignment:

Finally the answer was clear. Statistically, there are 486,000 youth in foster care in the United States, 50% of them have graduated from high school, and only 4% of them go to a four-year college.

"Shakila, you are valuable, you are loved; I want you to have not only a career, but a family as well. I want to bless you with a family, I want your dreams to come true, but I needed to build your character and I want you to help youth in foster care by letting them know that they can overcome like you did as well." This was God's message for me. So, there you go. God brought me all the way from Chicago, Illinois to Los Angeles, California, to fulfill my dream and walk in my destiny. Who knew that God's plan for our life is to have it all: Ministry, family and a career? With men, this is **impossible**, but with Christ, all things are **possible** (Matthew 19:26). Once I found my purpose, breakthrough happened for my company and me because I was using it for what it was created for. I didn't have to compromise my integrity to become successful.

I am a warrior, and Queen, and so are you. The Webster's Dictionary describes a Fighter as a "Warrior/soldier, someone that does not give up, someone who continues fighting or trying." You are a winner and you got this. Writing this book was an act of obedience from God. I was scared. Before I began to write, I had to look in the mirror and remind myself, "Chin up, shoulders back, happy face. You got this!" I prayed that the Lord would anoint my words and that they would help women walk in confidence towards their destiny. I hope it will bless you to walk towards your purpose in Christ. You got this. Nothing in this world is worth your destiny! Fight for yourself; surround yourself with the right people. Never give up. Chin up; you got this!

The end.

Chin Up! You Got This!

Shakila Stewart

Made in the USA
Las Vegas, NV
27 July 2021